AAT

Principles of Costing

Pocket Notes

These Pocket Notes support study for the following AAT qualifications:
AAT Certificate in Accounting – Level 2
AAT Certificate in Bookkeeping – Level 2
AAT Certificate in Accounting at SCQF Level 5

British library cataloguing-in-publication data

A catalogue record for this book is available from the British Library.

Published by:
Kaplan Publishing UK
Unit 2 The Business Centre
Molly Millars Lane
Wokingham
Berkshire
RG41 2QZ

ISBN 978-1-83996-903-4

© Kaplan Financial Limited, 2024

Printed and bound in Great Britain.

The text in this material and any others made available by any Kaplan Group company does not amount to advice on a particular matter and should not be taken as such. No reliance should be placed on the content as the basis for any investment or other decision or in connection with any advice given to third parties. Please consult your appropriate professional adviser as necessary. Kaplan Publishing Limited and all other Kaplan group companies expressly disclaim all liability to any person in respect of any losses or other claims, whether direct, indirect, incidental, consequential or otherwise arising in relation to the use of such materials.

All rights reserved. No part of this publication may be reproduced, stored in a retrieval system, or transmitted, in any form or by any means, electronic, mechanical, photocopying, recording or otherwise, without the prior written permission of Kaplan Publishing.

Principles of Costing

CONTENTS

		Study text chapter	Page Number
A guide to the assessment			1
Chapter 1	Introduction to costing systems	1	3
Chapter 2	Cost classification	2	9
Chapter 3	Materials and inventory	3	19
Chapter 4	Labour costs	4	27
Chapter 5	Overheads	5	33
Chapter 6	Budgeting and variances	6	39
Chapter 7	Introduction to spreadsheets	7	47
Index			I.1

Preface

These Pocket Notes contain the key things that you need to know for the exam, presented in a unique visual way that makes revision easy and effective.

Written by experienced lecturers and authors, these Pocket Notes break down content into manageable chunks to maximise your concentration.

Quality and accuracy are of the utmost importance to us so if you spot an error in any of our products, please send an email to mykaplanreporting@kaplan.com with full details, or follow the link to the feedback form in MyKaplan.

Our Quality Co-ordinator will work with our technical team to verify the error and take action to ensure it is corrected in future editions.

A guide to the assessment

A guide to the assessment

The assessment

The assessment will be in a single section.

Expect to see 7 independent tasks, several broken down into more than one requirement.

Learners will be assessed by computer based assessment (CBA) and will be required to demonstrate competence across the entire assessment.

The time allowed for this assessment is **90 minutes**.

Learning outcomes & weighting

1. Understand the cost recording system within an organisation — 30%
2. Use cost recording techniques — 40%
3. Provide information on actual and budgeted costs and income — 20%
4. Use tools and techniques to support cost calculations — 10%

Total — 100%

Pass mark

The pass mark for the unit assessment is 70%

chapter 1

Introduction to costing systems

- Financial accounting and management accounting.
- The aims of management accounting.
- Cost accounting.
- Terminology – cost units and cost centres.

Financial Accounting and Management Accounting

Characteristic	Financial Accounting	Management Accounting
Looks mainly at historical information.	✓	
Can include future forecasts and budgets.		✓
Formats dictated by accounting rules.	✓	
Content can include anything useful.		✓
Produced for shareholders and other external users.	✓	
Produced to help managers run the business.		✓
Produced in full once a year (and in some cases every 6 months).	✓	
Typically produced on a monthly basis.		✓
Based on historical cost information	✓	

The aims of management accounting

Aims of management information

Managers use information to help with:

Decision making — Such as which products to make, how much material to order, how many staff to employ, what selling price to set.

Planning — Preparing budgets and forecasts for a forthcoming period.

Controlling — Comparing actual results against budgets and taking corrective action where necessary to control costs.

Introduction to costing systems

Cost accounting

Definition

Cost accounting is the process of calculating and recording the costs involved in the production and distribution of products and services.

Main reason for carrying out cost accounting: to calculate the cost of a product and therefore set the sales price of the item.

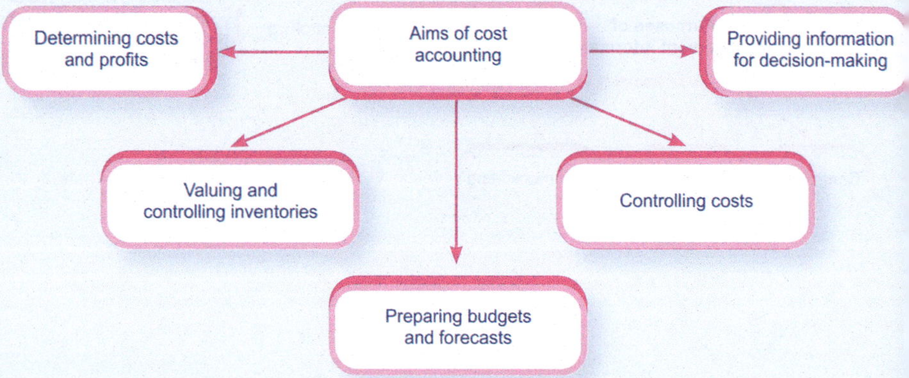

- Aims of cost accounting
  - Determining costs and profits
  - Providing information for decision-making
  - Valuing and controlling inventories
  - Controlling costs
  - Preparing budgets and forecasts

Terminology – cost units and cost centres

Cost unit = an individual unit for which the costs can be seperately identified.

Responsibility accounting is based on identifying individual parts of a business which are the responsibility of a single manager. There are four types of responsibility centre:

Cost centre = area of business for which costs will be separately ascertained.

Revenue centre = area of a business for which revenues will be separately ascertained.

Profit centre = area of business for which costs and revenues are ascertained.

Investment centre = area of business where costs, revenues and net assets are ascertained.

Example

Cost centres

- Manufacturing organisation
  - Production cost centres
    - Assembly line
    - Finishing
    - Packaging
  - Service cost centres
    - Stores
    - Maintenance
    - Quality control

Introduction to costing systems

chapter 2

Cost classification

- Cost classification:
  - overview.
  - by function.
  - by element.
  - by nature.
  - by behaviour.
- Coding systems.
- Product and period costs.

Cost classification – overview

Purpose	Classification
Financial accounts	By function • cost of sales • distribution costs • admin expenses • finance costs.
Cost control	By element • materials • labour • overheads.
Cost accounts	By nature • direct • indirect.
Budgeting, decision making	By behaviour • fixed • variable • semi-variable • stepped.

CBA focus

Make sure you understand the different types of cost classification as this is a very common exam requirement.

Cost classification – by function

Cost	Production = cost of sales	Distribution	Admin	Finance
Production labour	✓			
Production materials	✓			
Production supervisor salaries	✓			
Depreciation of factory equipment	✓			
Factory rent	✓			
Selling and distribution costs		✓		
Sales team commission		✓		
Delivery costs		✓		
Depreciation of delivery vehicles		✓		
Head office costs			✓	
IT support			✓	
HR support			✓	
Depreciation of head office equipment			✓	
Bank interest and charges				✓

Cost classification

Cost classification – by element

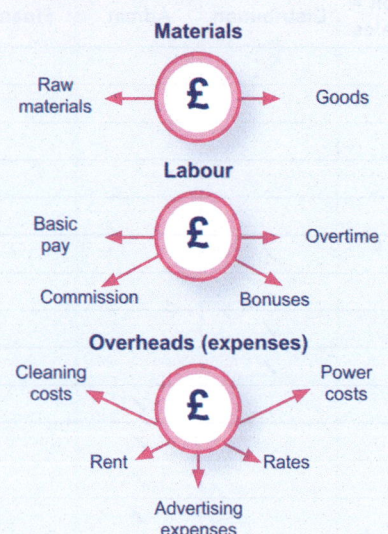

Cost classification – by nature

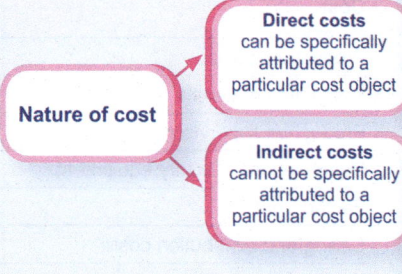

PRIME COST = direct material cost + direct labour cost + direct expenses

Indirect costs are also known as OVERHEADS

Cost classification – by behaviour

> A **variable cost** increases in total as the level of activity increases.

Graph of total variable cost

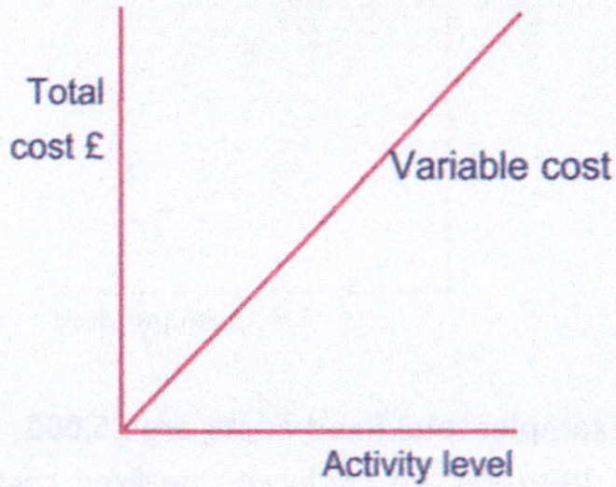

(Graph: Total cost £ on y-axis, Activity level on x-axis, showing an upward-sloping line labelled "Variable cost")

> A **variable cost** remains constant per unit as the level of activity increases.

Graph of unit variable cost

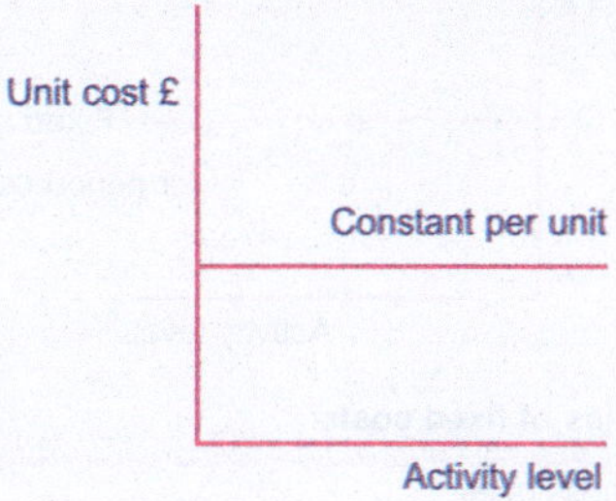

(Graph: Unit cost £ on y-axis, Activity level on x-axis, showing a horizontal line labelled "Constant per unit")

Examples of variable costs:

- Direct materials
- Direct labour

Cost classification

> A **fixed cost** does not increase as the level of activity increases.

Graph of total fixed cost

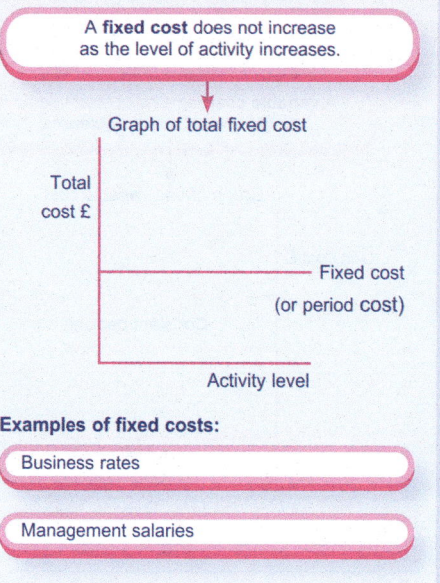

Examples of fixed costs:

- Business rates
- Management salaries

> A **fixed cost** reduces per unit as the level of activity increases.

Graph of fixed cost per unit

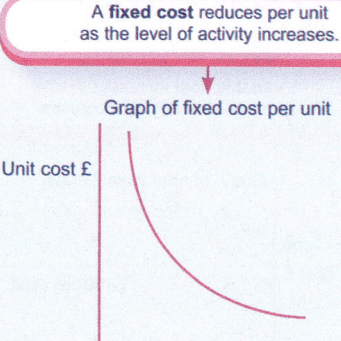

Example: total fixed costs are £5,000

If 100 units are produced, the fixed cost per unit is £50

If 500 units are produced, the fixed cost per unit is £10

A **semi-variable cost** is one that contains both fixed and variable elements.

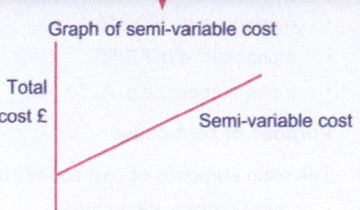

Semi-variable costs are also known as **semi-fixed costs** or **mixed costs**.

Examples of semi-variable costs:

Electricity costs – standing charge (fixed cost)
– cost per unit used (variable cost)

Salesperson's salary – basic (fixed) + bonus (variable)

A **stepped cost** is one that remains fixed over a certain range of activity, but increases if activity increases beyond that level.

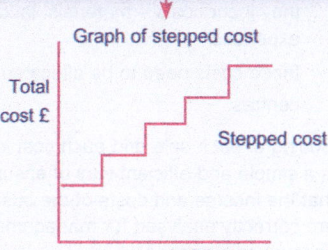

Examples of stepped costs:

Inventory storage costs

Supervisor salaries

Coding systems

- businesses make sales of various types/products and in different geographical regions
- they incur costs – materials, labour, expenses
- these costs need to be allocated to cost centres.

Coding of each sale and each cost incurred is a simple and efficient way of ensuring that the income and costs of the business are correctly analysed for management accounting purposes.

Types of code

There are a number of different methods of coding data:

- numeric: e.g. 100/310
- alphabetic: e.g. AB/RT
- alpha-numeric: e.g. A230

Purpose of cost codes

The main purposes of cost codes are to:

- assist precise information
- facilitate electronic data processing
- facilitate a logical and systematic arrangement of costing records
- simplify comparison of totals of similar expenses
- incorporate check codes.

Example

Coding purchase invoices

A manufacturing organisation has the following coding system for costs:

Cost centre	Code
Machining	101
Finishing	102
Packing	103
Maintenance	104
Office	105

Classification	Code
Material	121
Labour	122
Expense	123

Specific	Code
Oil	131
Steel	132
Plastic	133

An invoice is received for steel used in the machining department.

Code   101 121 132

CBA focus

In the assessment for Principles of Costing you may be given information which explains an organisation's coding system. Make sure that you read this carefully so that when you have to code documents or check coding done by others you fully understand how the particular coding system works.

Product and period costs

Product costs – charged to the individual product and matched against the sales revenue they generate in the period in which they are sold. These would include direct material, direct labour and absorbed production overheads, as showing in the cost card below.

Period costs – costs which are charged in full to the statement of profit or loss in the period in which they are incurred. These include costs such as administrative costs, selling and distribution costs and finance costs.

The cost card

A cost card is used to show the breakdown of the costs of producing output based on the classification of each cost. For example

Direct costs

Direct materials (3kg @ £5 per kg)	1
Direct labour (4 hours @ £10 per hour)	4
Direct expenses	1
Prime cost (total of direct costs)	6
Overheads (indirect costs)	1
Total product cost	8

chapter 3

Materials and inventory

- Different types of inventory.
- Valuing raw materials.
- Manufacturing accounts.
- Inventory control.

Materials and inventory

Different types of inventory

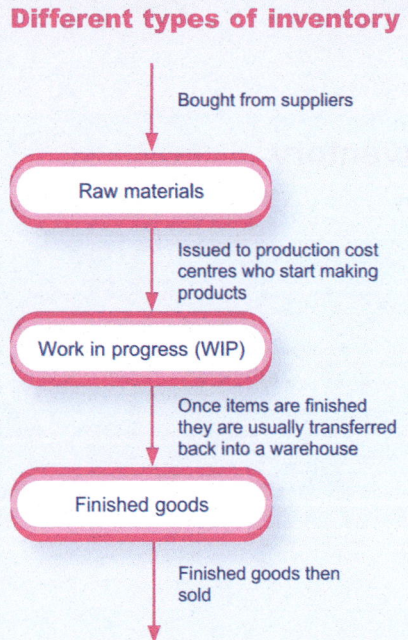

Why value inventory?

- **Costing.** To determine the cost of material issues to production cost centres, to include on the cost card for the cost unit.

- **Financial reporting.** To value the inventory left in stores at the end of the reporting period, to include in the financial statements.

Valuing raw materials

FIFO (First in, first out)

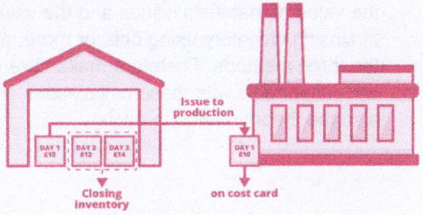

- Assumes that the issues to production will be made from the oldest inventory available leaving the most recent purchases in inventory.
- When prices are rising, FIFO will value closing inventory at a higher value and give a higher profit figure than LIFO or AVCO.
- Most suitable where goods are perishable, for example a dairy which produces milk.

LIFO (Last in, first out)

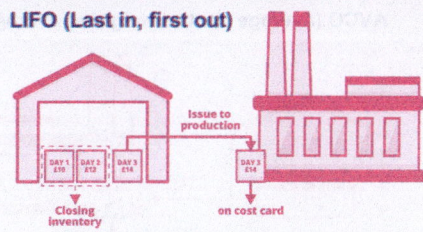

- Assumes that the issues to production will be made from the newest inventory available leaving the oldest purchases in inventory.
- When prices are rising, LIFO will value closing inventory at a lower figure and will give a lower profit figure than FIFO or AVCO.
- Most suitable when goods are not perishable, for example a builders merchant, where inventories of sand and bricks are stored in huge piles and it is not feasible to issue the oldest from the bottom of the pile.
- Not acceptable by HMRC or IAS 2.

AVCO (average cost or weighted average)

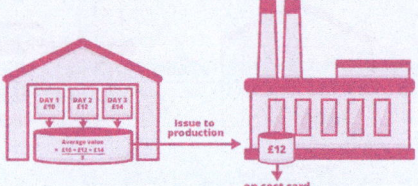

- Assumes that the issues to production will be made at an average price:

  Average price per unit = $\dfrac{\text{Total value of inventory}}{\text{Total units in inventory}}$

- A new average cost is calculated before each issue to production.
- AVCO could be used when individual units of material are not separately definable e.g, liquids, such as petrol.

CBA focus

A common assessment task is to calculate the value of materials issues and the value of closing inventory using one, or more, of the three methods. Therefore make sure you are comfortable with these calculations and also the theory related to each.

Chapter 3

Example

Swall Ltd has the following movements in a certain type of inventory into and out of it stores for the month of May:

Date	Receipts			Issues	
	Kg	Price / Kg	Cost	Kg	Cost
May 1	200	£4.50	£900		
May 2	100	£5.40	£540		
May 3				50	

Complete the table below for the issue and closing inventory values.

Method	Cost of issue	Closing inventory
FIFO		
LIFO		
AVCO		

Solution

Method	Cost of issue	Closing inventory
FIFO	£225	£1,215
LIFO	£270	£1,170
AVCO	£240	£1,200

Workings

FIFO

- The 50kg issued on the 3rd May will all come from the earliest purchase made on the 1st May.
- Thus the cost of the issue will be 50kg@£4.50 = £225
- Total purchases = £1,440, so closing inventory = 1,440 − 225 = £1,215

LIFO

- The 50kg issued on the 3rd May will all come from the most recent purchase made on the 2nd May.
- Thus the cost of the issue will be 50kg@£5.40 = £270
- Closing inventory = 1,440 − 270 = £1,170

AVCO

- We bought 300kg at a total cost of 900 + 540 = £1,440
- On average this works out at 1,440/300 = £4.80/kg
- Thus the cost of the issue will be 50kg@£4.80 = £240
- Closing inventory = 1,440 − 240 = £1,200

Manufacturing accounts

A manufacturing account shows how the costs of producing the finished goods that are sold during an accounting period has built up, i.e. cost of goods sold.

There are five main sections in a manufacturing account which you need to learn. These are highlighted in bold in the example here.

CBA focus

You need to know the order of the sections of the manufacturing account and which costs are included within each section (remember the adjustments for opening and closing inventories). An assessment question might also require the use of the interactive screen and spreadsheet functions for questions on this topic.

Example

Factory cost of goods sold

	£
Opening inventory of raw materials	7,000
Purchases of raw materials	50,000
Closing inventory of raw materials	(10,000)
DIRECT MATERIALS USED	**47,000**
Direct labour	97,000
DIRECT COST	**144,000**
Manufacturing overheads	53,000
MANUFACTURING COST	**197,000**
Opening inventory of work in progress	8,000
Closing inventory of work in progress	(10,000)
COST OF GOODS MANUFACTURED	**195,000**
Opening inventory of finished goods	30,000
Closing inventory of finished goods	(25,000)
COST OF GOODS SOLD	**200,000**

Inventory control

Functions of inventory

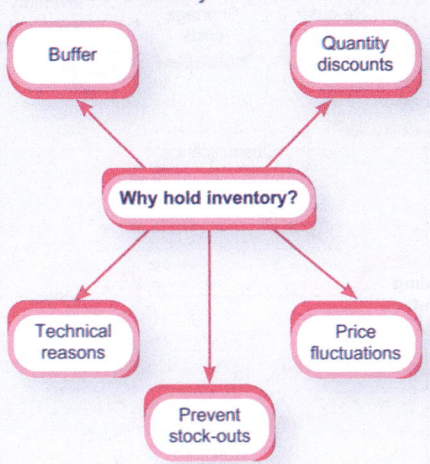

Inventory control

Definition

Inventory control: the method of ensuring that the right quantity of the right quality of the relevant inventory is available at the right time and in the right place.

The aim is to keep the costs of holding inventory down, whilst minimising the chances of stock-outs.

Control methods include:

- Buffer inventory
- Reorder level
- Reorder quantity
- Economic order quantity (EOQ)

CBA focus

In the exam, inventory control compliance will not be tested numerically, only in a discursive manner.

Materials and inventory

Holding costs

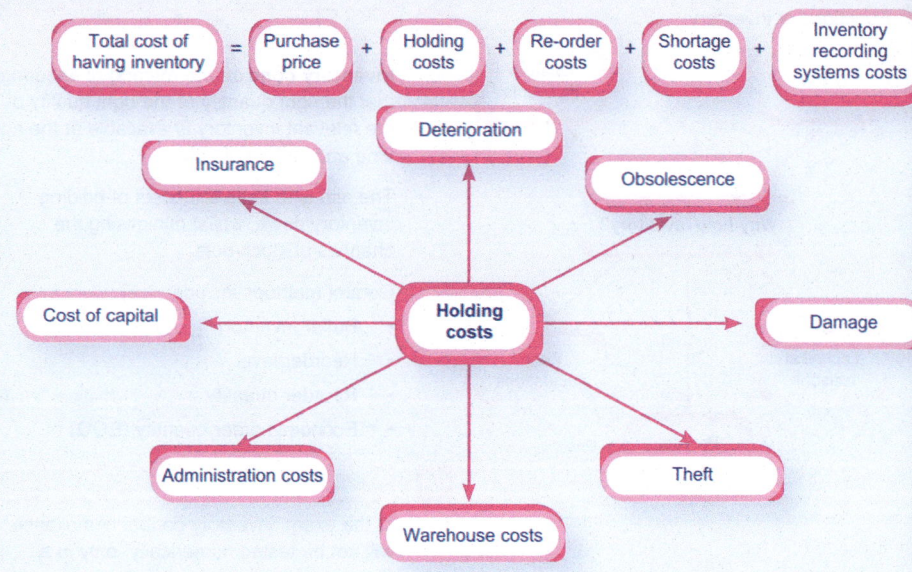

chapter 4

Labour costs

- Time related pay.
- Output related pay.
- Bonus schemes.

Time related pay

- Labour is paid according to the time spent at work / hours worked.
- Assured level of remuneration for employees.

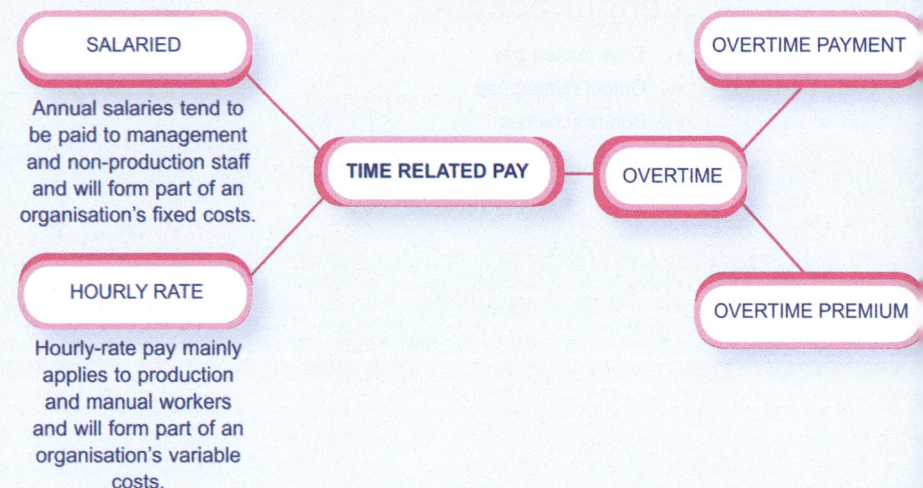

Example

Court works a standard week of 40 hours at an hourly rate of £8.20 per hour. Overtime is paid at time and a half.

Last week Court worked 45 hours.

Gross pay

Basic pay = 40 x £8.20 =	£328.00
Overtime = 5 x (£8.20 x 1.5) =	£61.50
Gross pay	£389.50

Overtime payment

Overtime hours = 45 – 40 = 5 hours

Overtime rate per hour = £8.20 x 1.5 = £12.30

Overtime payment = 5 hours x £12.30 = £61.50

Overtime premium

Overtime premium is the amount paid over the basic hourly rate for the overtime hours

Overtime premium
per hour = 0.5 x £8.20 = £4.10

Overtime hours = 5

Overtime premium = 5 hours x £4.10 = £20.50

Labour costs

Output related pay

- Labour is paid based on production output achieved.
- Employees earn more if they work more efficiently than expected.

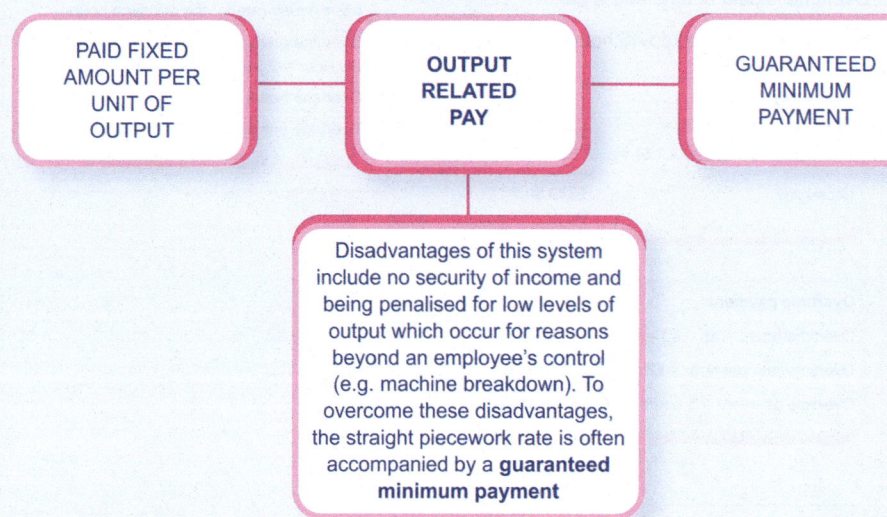

Bonus schemes

Bonuses may be paid to employees for a number of reasons:

- Individual performance
- Group performance
- Organisational performance.

The bonus calculation will differ for employees paid by results and employees paid on a time rate. It may be based on:

- Production above a certain standard level
- Time saved in relation to a standard time for production.

Bonus cap:

Where a bonus is paid for achieving a certain level of output, companies may place a **'cap'** on the bonus, meaning it is only paid up to a certain level of output.

e.g.

A company pays a bonus of £2 for every unit of output where output exceeds 350 units in a week, capped at 500 units.

If an employee produced 550 units, the bonus would only be paid for units 351-500 (and not for units 501-550). Total bonus would be capped at 150 units x £2 = £300.

chapter 5

Overheads

- Overheads.
- Overhead absorption.
- Total and unit costs.

Overheads

In a previous chapter we saw how the total unit cost of a product or service is made up of direct costs plus indirect costs, or **'overheads'**.

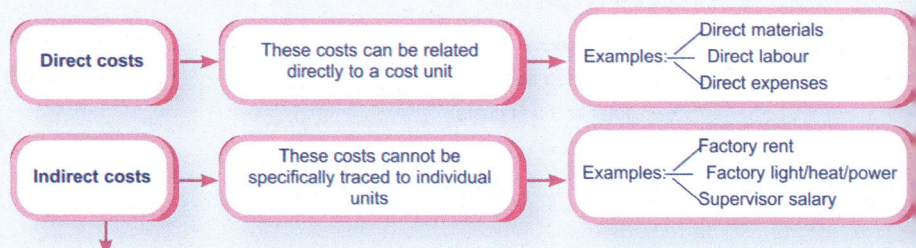

Also known as **overheads**

- **Production overheads** may be accounted for as part of cost of sales (factory rent, insurance, light and heat costs). This chapter focuses on production overheads and relating these costs to products.
- **Non-production overheads** may be accounted for below the gross profit line (administrative costs, selling and distribution costs).

Overhead absorption

Key Point

The charging of overhead costs to cost units is called **overhead absorption**.

Absorption rate bases

Various overhead absorption rates exist and the most suitable one should be selected. The use of an absorption rate per unit is for one-product businesses but the following bases may be more appropriate for a multi-product business:

- Absorption rate per direct labour hour
- Absorption rate per direct machine hour.

Direct labour hour rates are commonly used in labour-intensive production whereas direct machine hour rates are commonly used in machine-intensive production.

- Calculated at the start of a period
- Based on budgets (estimates)

$$\text{Overhead absorption rate} = \frac{\text{Budgeted overheads}}{\text{Budgeted activity levels}}$$

Overheads

Example

Overhead absorption rates

Sunshine Ltd estimates that the total factory costs for the coming year will be as follows:

	£
Direct materials	40,000
Direct wages	60,000
Prime cost	100,000
Factory overhead	30,000
Total factory cost	130,000

The factory will produce 10,000 units of a variety of different products.

It is anticipated that during the year there will be 30,000 direct labour hours worked and 15,000 machine hours.

Rate per unit $= \dfrac{\text{Budgeted overheads}}{\text{Budgeted production}}$

$= \dfrac{£30,000}{10,000 \text{ units}} = £3 \text{ per unit}$

Rate per direct labour hour

$= \dfrac{\text{Budgeted overheads}}{\text{Budgeted direct labour hours}}$

$= \dfrac{£30,000}{30,000 \text{ hours}} = £1 \text{ per labour hour}$

Rate per machine hour

$= \dfrac{\text{Budgeted overheads}}{\text{Budgeted machine hours}}$

$= \dfrac{£30,000}{15,000 \text{ hours}} = £2 \text{ per machine hour}$

Total and unit costs

Within this unit you will need to be able to calculate total and unit costs at different activity levels.

You need to remember to distinguish between variable costs and fixed costs

- Fixed costs remain constant for each activity level.
- Variable costs increase in line with activity levels.

Complete the table below showing budgeted fixed costs, variable costs, total costs and unit cost at the different possible budgeted levels of production:

Example

Units	Fixed costs £	Variable Costs £	Total Costs £	Unit Cost £
200	10,000	8,000	18,000	90.00
400				
600				

Overheads

Solution:

Units	Fixed costs £	Variable Costs £	Total Costs £	Unit Cost £
200	10,000	8,000	18,000	90.00
400	10,000	16,000	26,000	65.00
600	10,000	24,000	34,000	56.67

Workings:

Fixed costs remain the same for each activity level.

Variable costs per unit are found by taking total variable costs for 200 units and dividing by 200 units = £8,000/200 units = £40 per unit.

Variable costs for 400 units = £40 x 400 = £16,000.

Variable costs for 600 units = £40 x 600 = £24,000.

Total costs = fixed costs + variable costs.

Unit cost = total costs / number of units.

chapter 6

Budgeting and variances

- The purpose of budgets.
- Types of budget.
- Variances.
- Significance of variances.
- Causes of variances.

The purpose of budgets

Definition

A budget is a quantitative expression of a plan of action prepared in advance of the period to which it relates.

- Budgets set out the costs and revenues that are expected to be incurred or earned in future periods.

Budgetary control

Two of the main reasons for budgeting are to help managers with planning and control of the business.

- **Planning**: The budgeting process forces managers to look ahead, set targets and plan for the future. The budget provides a benchmark against which actual performance can be measured.

- **Control**: Any difference between actual results and the budget (known as a variance) can then be investigated to identify the cause. Once we know this we can take appropriate action.

BUDGETS
- Co-ordinating activities
- Planning for the future
- Communication of targets
- Controlling costs
- Motivation
- Authorisation of expenditure
- Performance evaluation

Types of budget

Definition

A **fixed budget** is a budget produced for a **single** activity level.

Fixed budgets:

- remain unchanged even if actual activity is different
- therefore, do not compare like with like
- therefore, do not assist in identifying the cause of variances.

Definition

A **flexible (or flexed) budget** is a budget which, by recognising cost behaviour patterns, is designed to change as volume of activity changes.

- comparing a flexible budget with actual results provides management with more meaningful information.

CBA focus

In your exam you may be required to prepare a fixed budget for a single product organisation, using unit cost information. You may also need to use an interactive table, simulating a spreadsheet, in order to do this.

Variances

Variance = difference between actual figure and comparison figure.

Favourable variance = actual result better than comparison figure.

Adverse variance = actual results worse than comparison figure.

Note: here the comparison figure will be the budget.

An example of a variance statement

	Budget	Actual	Variance value	Favourable or Adverse	Variance percentage %
	£	£	£		
Sales Revenue	27,400	30,000	2,600	F	9.5
Direct Materials	3,425	3,875	450	A	13.1
Direct Labour	6,439	6,501	62	A	1.0
Fixed overheads	4,795	4,975	180	A	3.8
Profit	12,741	14,649	1,908	F	

Significance of a variances

Management do not want to waste time investigating small variances, so will set criteria for deciding what makes a variance large enough to report and investigate.

For example,
- 'Only investigate variances bigger than £500'.
- 'Only investigate variances bigger that 5% of budget'.

If using a percentage measure then the amount of the variance that exceeds the cut-off percentage is known as the 'discrepancy'.

$$\text{Variance as a \% of budget} = \frac{\text{variance}}{\text{budget}} \times 100$$

Reporting variances

It stands to reason that variances should be reported to the individual responsible for them happening, or who can take action on them.

For example, a Direct Materials cost variance that is due to materials price paid – report to Purchasing Manager.

Sales variance – report to Sales Manager.

Causes of variances

Differences between actual values and budgeted values can occur for a number of reasons. The main reason being that when we produce a budget we are trying to predict the future, which is not an exact science! Other reasons for variances could include:

Sales variances
- better quality product, therefore higher price
- more competition, therefore lower price
- more/fewer units sold than expected

Materials variance
- better/lower quality material, affecting the price paid
- more/less wastage than expected

Labour variances
- more/less trained staff being paid differing rates per hour
- work took more/less hours than expected

CBA focus

In the CBA you need to be able to do the following.

1. Calculate variances.
2. See whether they are favourable or adverse.
3. Assess whether they are significant.
4. Assess who variances should be reported to.
5. Identify possible causes and effects of variances.

Assessment tasks on this topic may also require the use of the interactive screen and spreadsheet functions.

Budgeting and variances

chapter 7

Introduction to spreadsheets

- Introduction to spreadsheets.
- Entering data.
- Formatting cells.
- Formatting numbers.
- Using formulas.

Introduction to spreadsheets

A spreadsheet is a computer file that consists of rows and columns that is used to manipulate data. It can be used to support the cost calculations that we have seen in previous chapters.

CBA focus

In your assessment, you will be presented with an interactive screen for the completion of some of the tasks. You will need to use the functions and formatting tools available on the screen to perform cost calculations and to format data, based on the syllabus content that has been covered in the previous chapters.

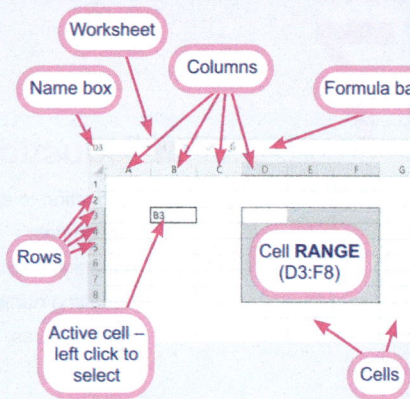

Entering data

To enter data into the active cell, simply type the data required into the cell – either numeric or text. As you type, the data will be displayed on the spreadsheet itself and within the formula bar.

Inserting rows and columns

Clicking this icon will give you the option to insert new rows or columns.

New rows will appear **above** the cell which is selected at the time.

New columns will appear to the **left** of the cell which is selected at the time.

Clicking this icon will give you the option to delete rows or columns.

The row or column of whichever is highlighted will be deleted.

Copy and paste

Highlight the cell you wish to copy the contents from.

Click the 'Copy' icon.

Select the cell you wish to copy the contents to.

Click the 'paste' icon.

Formatting cells

The formatting cells menu in Excel has many in-depth formatting capabilities. However, for the purpose of your assessment, the formatting tools that you will need will be found in the ribbon along the top of the interactive screen.

We will use the icons as they appear in Excel 2016 here, but these may be slightly different in your assessment.

Font formatting

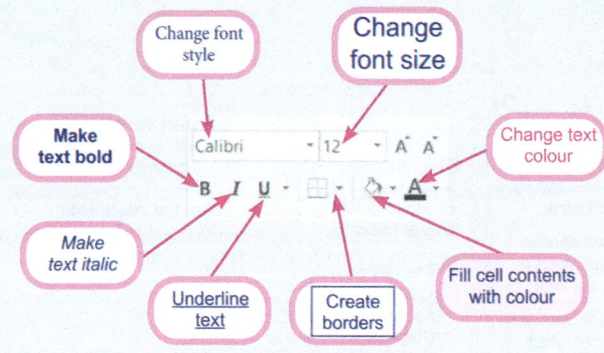

Alignment formatting tools:

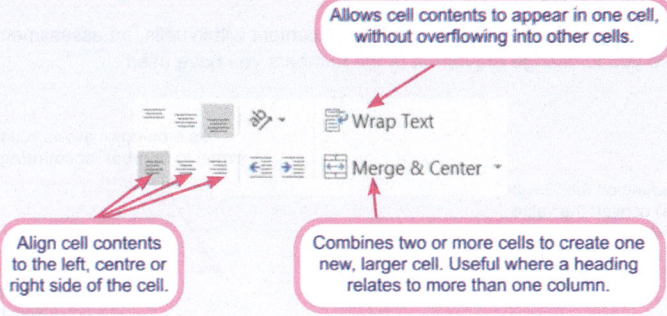

Introduction to spreadsheets

Formatting numbers

CBA focus

As well as changing the appearance of the text content within cells, an assessment question might also require you to change the format of the numbers you have used.

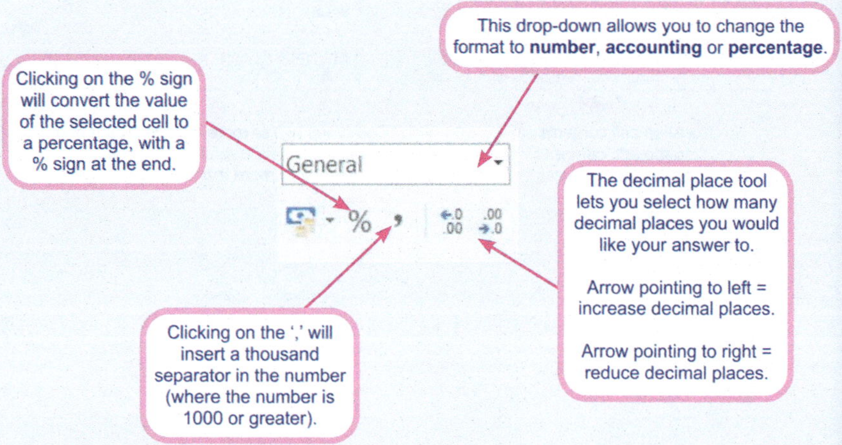

> This drop-down allows you to change the format to **number**, **accounting** or **percentage**.

> Clicking on the % sign will convert the value of the selected cell to a percentage, with a % sign at the end.

> The decimal place tool lets you select how many decimal places you would like your answer to.
>
> Arrow pointing to left = increase decimal places.
>
> Arrow pointing to right = reduce decimal places.

> Clicking on the ',' will insert a thousand separator in the number (where the number is 1000 or greater).

Using formulas

CBA focus

One of the tasks in your assessment will require you to use formulas within the interactive screen in order to arrive at the correct solution.

Addition

To add individual cells:

=number1+number2, e.g.=A3+B8
=SUM(number1,[number2]), e.g. =SUM(A3,B8)
To add a range of cells:
=SUM(number1:number2), e.g. =SUM(A3:B8)

Subtraction

=number1-number2, e.g. =B8-A3

Multiplication

=number1*number2, e.g. =A3*B8

Division

=number1/number2, e.g. =B8/A3

Introduction to spreadsheets

Index

Index

A

Absorption 35
Absorption rate 35
Adverse variance 42
Assigning responsibility for variances 43
AVCO 22

B

Bonus cap 31
Bonus schemes 31
Budget 40
Budgetary control 40
Budgets 40

C

Causes of variances 44
Coding systems 16, 17
Cost accounting 6
Cost card 18
Cost centre 7
Cost classification by behaviour 13, 15
Cost classification by element 12
Cost classification by function 11
Cost classification by nature 12
Cost classification overview 18
Cost units and centres 7

D

Direct expenses 34

F

Factory cost of goods sold 24
Favourable variance 42
FIFO 21
Financial accounting and management accounting 4
Finished goods 20
Fixed budget 41
Fixed costs 14
Flexible budget 41
Formatting cells 50
Formatting numbers 52
Formulas 53

Index

G
Guaranteed minimum payment 30

H
Holding costs 26

I
Indirect costs 34
Indirect expenses 34
Inventory control 25
Investment centre 7

L
LIFO 21

M
Management accounting aims 5
Manufacturing accounts 24

N
Non-production overheads 34

O
Output related pay 30
Overhead absorption rates 35, 36
Overheads 34
Overtime payment 28, 29
Overtime premium 28, 29

P
Product and period costs 18
Production overheads 34
Profit centre 5, 7
Purpose of budgets 40
Purpose of cost codes 16

R
Raw materials 20
Reporting variances 43
Responsibility centres 7
Revenue centre 7

Index

S

Salaried pay 28
Semi-variable cost 15
Semi-variable costs 15
Significance of a variances 43
Spreadsheets 48, 49
Stepped costs 15

T

Time related pay 28
Total and unit costs 37, 38

V

Valuing wip and finished goods 21
Variable costs 13
Variance percentage 43
Variances 42

W

Work in progress (WIP) 20